MAYA DESIGNS

Wilson G. Turner

Dover Publications, Inc.
New York

Dedicated to

G. ELIZABETH TURNER

With thanks to Beverley Trupe and John Rafter
for their encouragement and assistance.

Maya Designs, as published by Dover Publications, Inc., in 1985, is a
slightly revised publication incorporating all the designs of the work originally published by Dover in 1980 under the title *Maya Design Coloring
Book*.

DOVER *Pictorial Archive* SERIES

International Standard Book Number: 0-486-24047-9

Manufactured in the United States of America
Dover Publications, Inc., 31 East 2nd Street, Mineola, N.Y. 11501

PUBLISHER'S NOTE

The ancient Maya civilization flourished for many centuries—from before the birth of Christ until the Spanish Conquest—in Guatemala, Honduras and adjoining parts of Mexico. After a long period of slow growth, the Maya classic period lasted approximately from 300 to 900 A.D. This was the golden age of the southern Maya centers such as Tikal (Guatemala), Yaxchilán and Palenque (both in the state of Chiapas, Mexico). Afterwards, the emphasis in Maya civilization moved north, into Yucatán and neighboring regions. There in the north, a second brilliant period or renaissance occurred from about 950 to 1200 A.D., the time of the greatness of such sites as Chichén Itzá and Kabah. During this later period, however, and during the decline that followed, Maya culture was heavily influenced, and even controlled, by the more powerful Toltecs of Mexico.

Objects created by the Maya include painted vases and other ceramics, architectural sculpture and other monumental carvings, murals, illustrated books and miscellaneous artifacts. Items in all these categories are represented in this book. All are outstanding authentic pieces in museums, private collections or still in their original sites; a few have been redrawn from illustrations in scholarly journals. The captions reflect the best current information on dating, identification of figures and other facts.

Many of the designs include glyphs; these pictorial characters, used to express words and ideas, were the elements of Maya writing. No key to them has been found, and only about ten percent of them have been deciphered. The meaning of several of these symbols has been given in the captions.

The Maya used color lavishly on their costumes, buildings and all other objects. The brilliant green tail feathers of the quetzal bird were not only revered but were used in headdresses and other clothing ornaments. Each of the cardinal directions was represented by a color. In the writings, glyphs could represent either the color itself or ideas associated with it: yellow stands for purity, green represents "new" as in new growth, turquoise can be "precious" or "water," white can mean "substitute," black can mean "real."

In working with these designs, you may wish to add color. The Maya themselves used several shades of yellow—such as lemon yellow, yellow orange and yellow ochre—and shades of brown from a reddish hue through yellowish to a very dark brown. Their blues ran into greens and their greens into blues, including turquoise. A few of the illustrations in the book appear in color on the covers as examples of what can be done.

This ball-court marker at Copán (a ruined city in western Honduras) is one of the three seen in the center of the playing field in the small drawing. Most Maya ritual centers had similar arenas of varying size and architecture. A similar ball game was played by all Indians from Arizona through Mexico to Central America. The game had religious connotations.

A sculptured lintel (Lintel 8 in Structure 1) from the ruins of Yaxchilán (in the state of Chiapas, Mexico, at the border with Guatemala) shows the warriors Bird Jaguar and Jeweled Skull taking captives on May 7, 755 A.D. Maya personages of rank are depicted larger than subordinates or slaves. More than half of the glyphs in this carving have been translated.

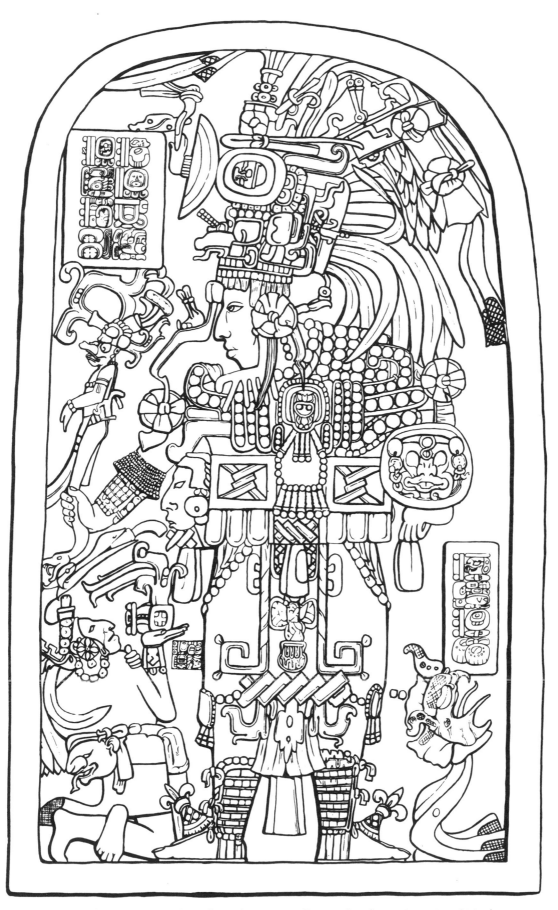

The stela, or stone marker, shown here originally stood in the ancient site of Macha-quila II in the Petén department of Guatemala. It was stolen, cut into 19 pieces and taken out of the country. Now restored to its original appearance and ownership, it is displayed at the Los Angeles County Museum of Art on indefinite loan from the government of Guatemala. A captive is seen offering yellow maize (the most pure food) to the large central figure.

Seated upon symbols for the moon, which represents the number 20, plus the bar and **dots** for the number 9, this scientist has a throne that totals to a full lunar cycle of 29 **days**. He is one of 20 or more figures, perhaps scientists assembled from many **centers**, that were on the steps to the inner doorway of the Temple of Inscriptions at **Copán.** (British Museum, London)

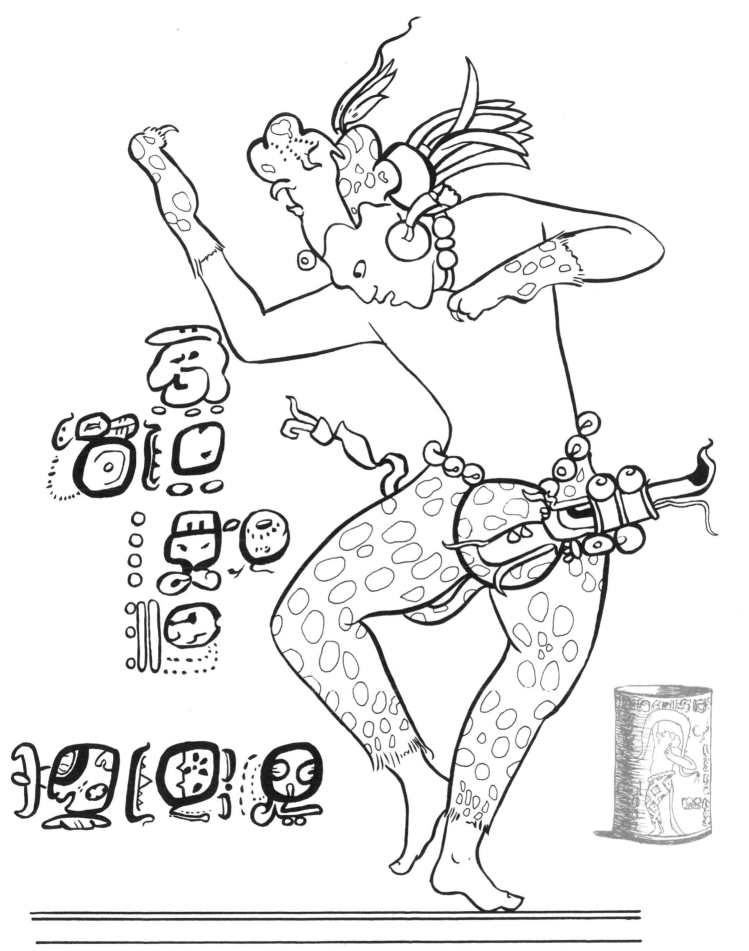

Decorating a ceramic funerary vase that held the ashes of a Maya priest or ruler, this jaguar dancer impersonates the jaguar god of the underworld. The picture was intended to aid the deceased after death. The small picture shows the reverse side of the same vase. (Peabody Museum, Harvard University)

The free-flowing design—typical of Maya ceramics—on this three-legged funerary bowl is in marked contrast to the structured motifs adorning objects of a more rigid nature. Like some North American Indians, the Maya sometimes punched a hole through the middle of a burial vessel to "kill" it before it was interred. (Private collection)

Page 13a of the *Dresden Codex,* one of three remaining Maya books. The gods of death, maize and the north (left to right), each holding the symbol for maize, are identified in the inscriptions above. Maya books were made to fold like a screen, as shown in the small picture.

This beautiful bas-relief plaque from Palenque (Chiapas, Mexico) is unusual in that it has no border, its perimeter being controlled only by the shape of the stone on which the work was carved. The main figure is receiving a headdress from an attendant. The two-headed jaguar throne is found a number of times in Maya works. (British Museum, London)

The figure in this bas-relief stone tablet from Palenque holds aloft a water lily, **symbol** of abundance. The glyph object on which he sits also refers to **this plant**. Although the Maya carved many pieces in the round, their real forte was **bas-relief**. (Museo de América, Madrid)

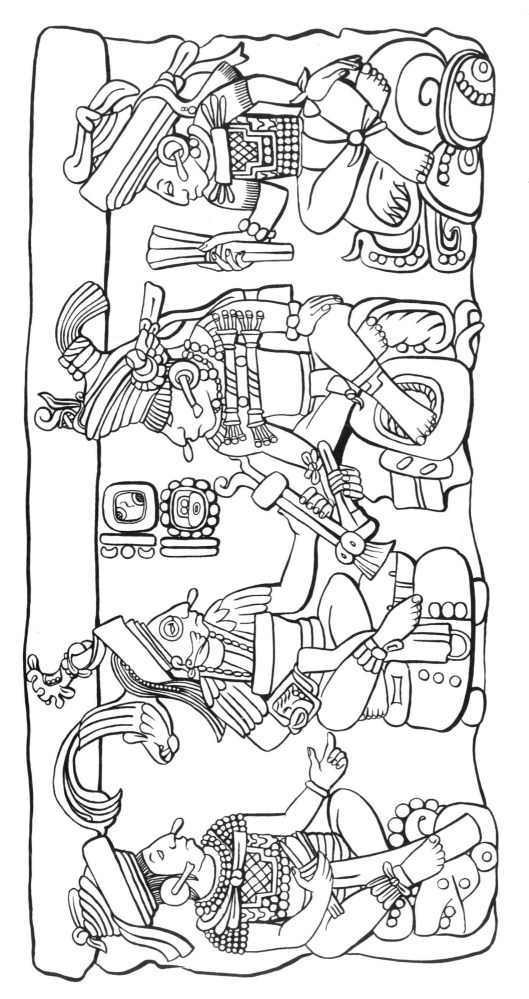

Archaeologists assume that the 16 men on Altar Q at Copán (the four shown here appear on the western face) are astronomers attending a great convention, around 776 A.D., to correct the Maya calendar. The altar is still located at Copán.

On the front panel of this vase from Ratinlixul, Guatemala, a merchant, who has taken his pet dog along, is traveling by litter. One of the additional porters laden with belongings and merchandise is carrying a paddle for fording waterways. The explorer John L. Stephens reported that the Maya were still traveling in this manner in 1842.

11

Tikal, an important early site in northern Guatemala, was the source of this lid from a funerary bowl (from Burial 10). The bowl, shown reassembled and complete in the inset, probably held the ashes of the deceased. It has been dated ca. 450 A.D. The figure represented is the Toltec god of spring. At this period the Toltec bowl would have been acquired through trade. Later the Toltecs, a Central Mexican group, traveled south, conquered much of the Maya area and established themselves firmly in Yucatán.

The Maya wrote numbers, weeks, months, years and similar concepts not only in abstract symbols but also with the images of certain gods that symbolized those concepts. In a very few cases, as in this segment from a carved stela still standing in Copán, there are full-figure glyphs in which the number god and the time-period god are entwined.

In this detail from a lintel in House F at Yaxchilán, the crosshatching serves two different purposes. In the figure at the right, it indicates the color black, as it normally does in Maya sculpture. In the robe of the other figure, however, it represents a woven pattern. (British Museum, London)

Maya sculptors worked principally with stone, but occasionally used bone, shell and wood. The large design on this page is on a carved peccary skull from Copán, which is shown in its entirety in the small drawing. (Peabody Museum, Harvard University)

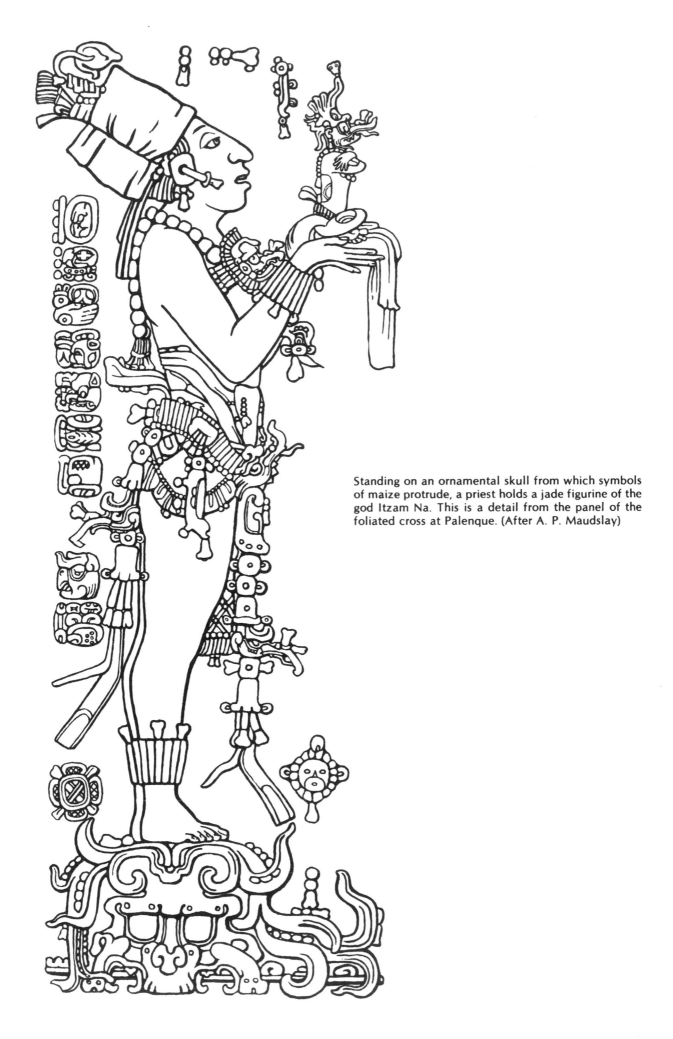

Standing on an ornamental skull from which symbols of maize protrude, a priest holds a jade figurine of the god Itzam Na. This is a detail from the panel of the foliated cross at Palenque. (After A. P. Maudslay)

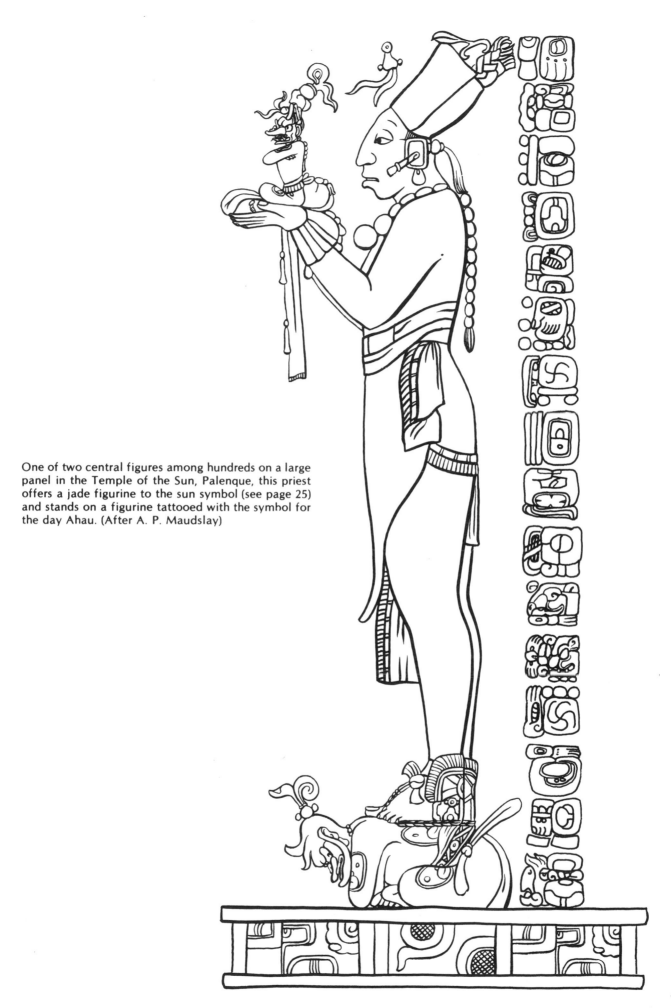

One of two central figures among hundreds on a large panel in the Temple of the Sun, Palenque, this priest offers a jade figurine to the sun symbol (see page 25) and stands on a figurine tattooed with the symbol for the day Ahau. (After A. P. Maudslay)

The many famed murals at Bonampak, Chiapas, Mexico, about 25 miles from Yax-chilán, are deteriorating rapidly. Outstanding copies have been made under the auspices of the Mexican government, and have been deposited in the Peabody Museum. This section of the north wall of Room 2, Structure 1, shows Maya warriors with captives from a raiding party.

Another of the three remaining Maya books is the *Madrid Codex*. The detail of page 97b adapted here illustrates the time of year for carving new masks. Chac, Itzam Na and the maize god are shown doing the carving. The glyph with three black dots above each of them is the one that means "new masks."

This mask of the long-nosed rain god Chac is one of hundreds adorning the facade of a building at Kabah, Yucatán. (A side view of the facade is shown in the inset.) Toltec designs like this ornamented many buildings in Yucatán after the Maya were conquered (around the year 1000 A.D.) by the Toltecs from Mexico.

In this group of glyphs from the back panel of a stela still at Copán, the wing-shaped border design represents feathers of the sacred quetzal bird. The inset shows the group in its position at the very bottom of the stela (which has a full-size carved figure on its front panel).

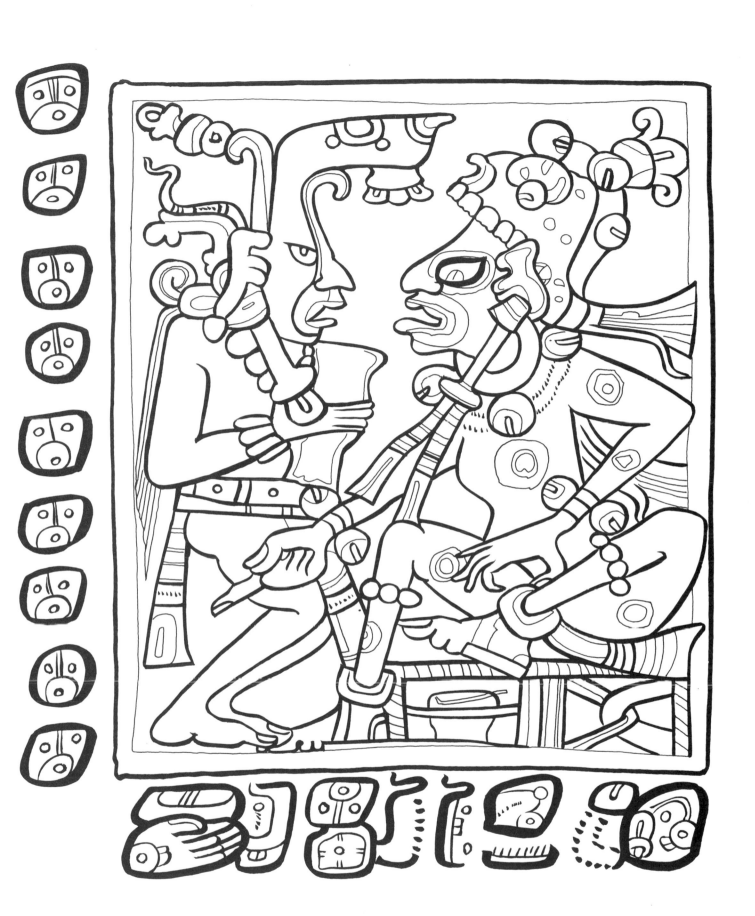

On page 50 of the *Dresden Codex* appear these two deities. The god of maize and life wears a necklace of jade beads and a headdress with the maize symbol. The god of death and disease wears copper bells and has spots on his body.

On the island of Jaina near Campeche, Mexico, was found this lovely small ocarina, made of clay in a press mold. Heads of gods protrude from serpents' mouths in the priest's headdress. (Museo Nacional de Antropología, Mexico City; from a photo by Ferdinand Anton)

The sun symbol at Palenque being worshipped by the priest seen on page 17 is suspended from crossed spears that rest on a platform decorated with three serpent heads. The platform itself rests on the backs of two priests, one wearing a jaguar skin, the other a costume of sky symbols. Water lilies (which stand for abundance) are shown at each corner of the solar disc. (After A. P. Maudslay)

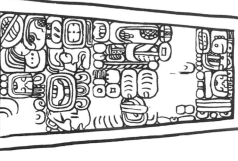

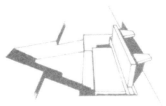

The throne from Piedras Negras, Guatemala, now in that country's Museo Nacional de Arqueologia, was originally carved for a stone niche, as shown in the inset. The facing human heads are framed by the eye sockets of a dragon-like monster that has bones protruding from its nostrils and ear plugs at the outer sides of its eyes. Where possible, damaged portions of the design have been restored in the drawing, but blank spaces have been left where glyphs are missing.

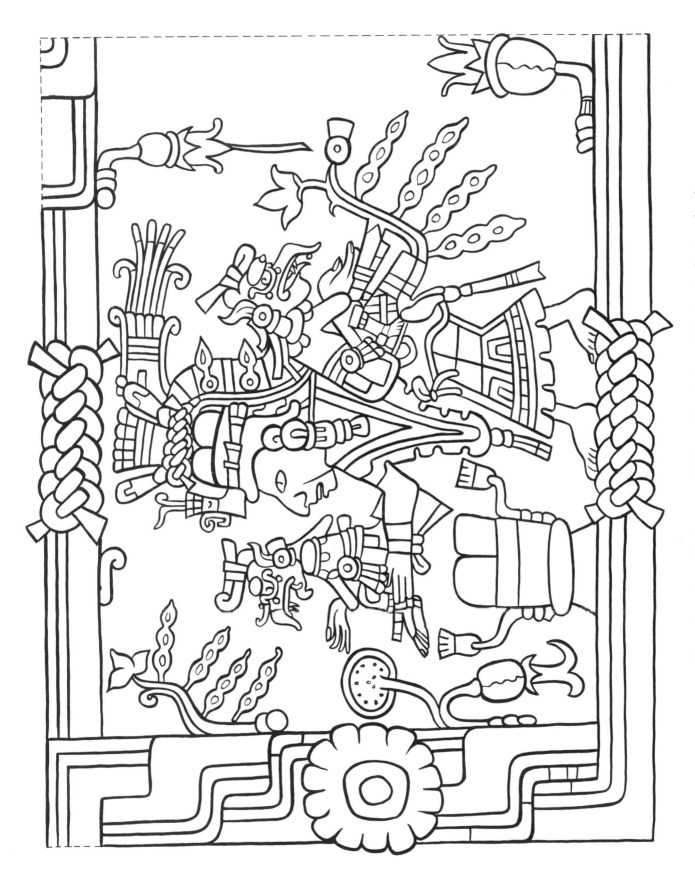

Among the earlier ruins at Tulum in the Quintana Roo territory of Mexico is the Temple of Frescos. This section from a mural in that building dates from about 110 A.D.

27

Still in its original location in Tikal is Altar 5, one of the most beautifully carved pieces at that site. Two elaborately dressed men kneel in conference beside a skull and a stack of thighbones.

The athlete on this ball-court marker from Chinkultic, Chiapas, Mexico, wears leather protectors around his waist and on his supporting leg.

A pendant carved on both sides, the Leiden Plate (or Plaque) is one of the earliest inscribed Maya artifacts. On one side are calendrical glyphs pointing to a date around 230 A.D.; on the other is a captive at the feet of a prince who wears bird, animal and human-head trophies on his belt and costume. Made at Tikal, this object is now at the Rijksmuseum van Oudheden, Leiden, Netherlands.

On Stela 10 from Seibal, in the Petén of Guatemala, dated 849 A.D., is a mustachioed ruler in full regalia, including a jaguar-skin skirt and sandals with ornamental pineapples. (From Peabody Museum photographs)

Above is another example of a glyph (this one from Palenque) consisting of a full figure instead of a stylized design or a head only (whether an animal's or some other being's). Compare page 13.

The jaguar was an important symbol to the Maya and was frequently used for various forms of decoration. This bas-relief was found in the walls of the Mausoleum Mound 13 at Chichén Itzá, Yucatán.

This funerary vessel from Palenque, now in the Los Angeles County Museum of Art, shows the sun god with blank eyes and a filed front tooth. His headdress and collar are composed of masks. The intricate designs and the wing panel behind the sculpture are typical. Traces of turquoise paint remain on many similar pieces, which were once brightly colored.

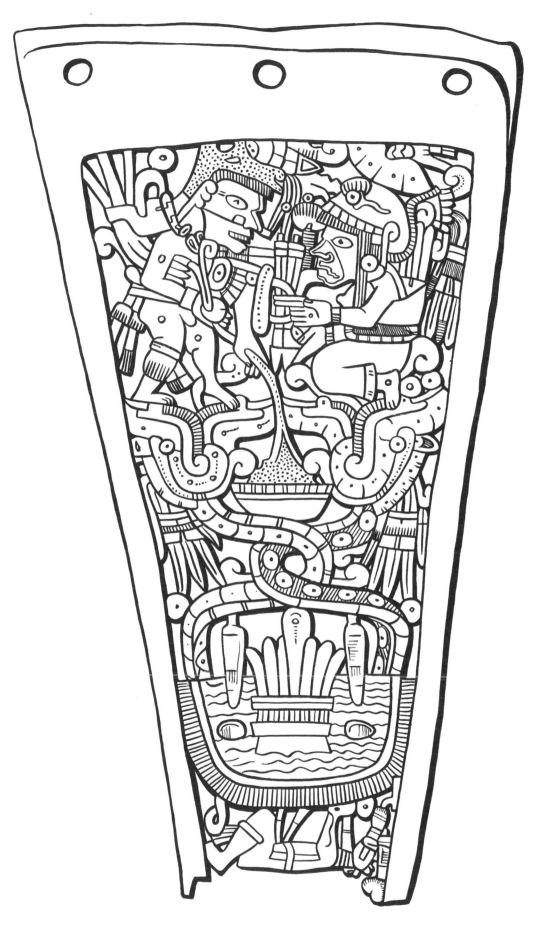

On this perforated shell ornament from the state of Veracruz, Mexico, two figures with entwined serpents are performing a ceremony while a small figure, on its back, supports the entire tableau. This very early piece, on the borderline of the Maya period, is now at the Middle American Research Institute, Tulane University, New Orleans.

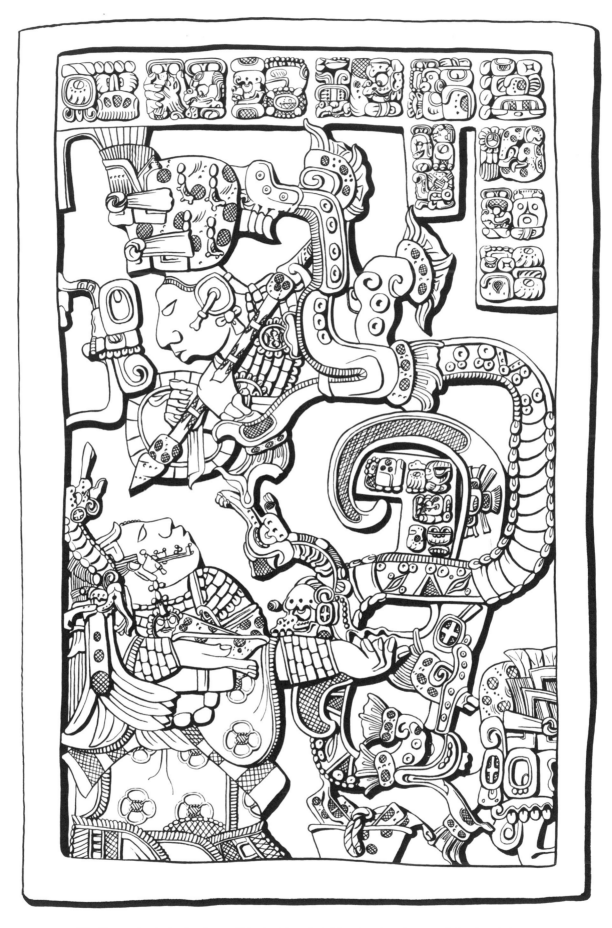

The first pair of glyphs above (5 Imix, 4 Mac) yield a date for this Yaxchilán lintel that corresponds to 681 A.D. Unlike most carvings in Maya, which read from left to right, the original of this stela is carved in the reverse direction, for some unexplained reason. So that the modern student can read the inscription, the artist has reversed the original, so the drawing reads from left to right.

Carved from a 7-by-12-foot limestone slab, this sarcophagus lid from Palenque covered the first Maya tomb found inside a pyramid. It depicts the great leader Pacal and religious symbols such as the venerated ceiba tree whose branches reach toward heaven, the two-headed sky dragon and celestial birds.

Page 27 b and c of the *Dresden Codex* depicts some of the Maya New Year ceremonies. The bowl at the top center contains the symbols "new" and "pure," also meaning "green" and "yellow," respectively. A bowl of maize and fish is shown in front of the god Itzam Na. Below, in front of the god of death, who holds a headless turkey, is a bowl of onions and another bowl of maize and fish.

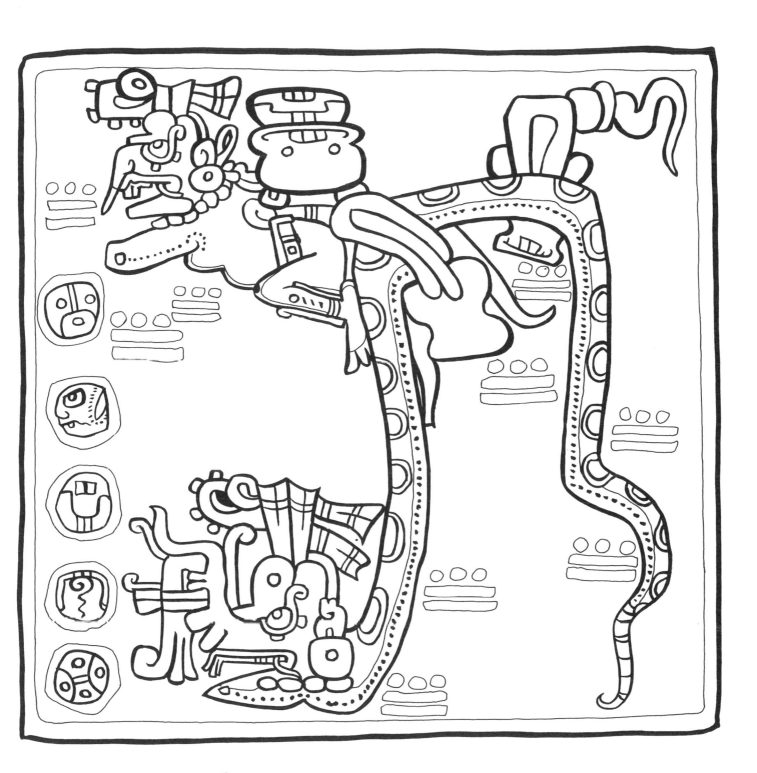

In a detail from page 31 of the *Madrid Codex*, a serpent supports the rain god Chac, who has a bowl of maize on his back. Each group of bars and dots forms the number 13. The five symbols at the far left are the day names (top to bottom) Ahau, Eb, Kan, Cib and Lamat.

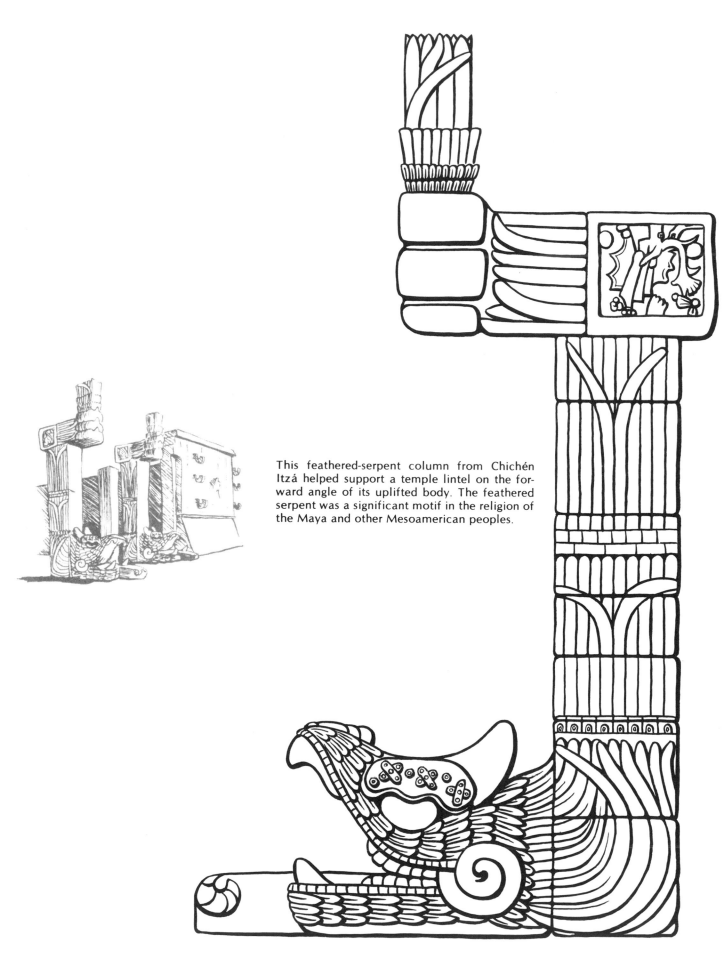

This feathered-serpent column from Chichén Itzá helped support a temple lintel on the forward angle of its uplifted body. The feathered serpent was a significant motif in the religion of the Maya and other Mesoamerican peoples.

Stela 3 from La Mar, Chiapas, Mexico, 795 A.D., depicts a chief grasping a captive. The stone, once broken, has been reassembled; damaged detail has been restored in the drawing. A copy of the stela is displayed at the Los Angeles County Museum of Art.